Many Cultures, One World

Greece

by Gina DeAngelis

Consultant:
Yiorgos Anagnostu, Assistant Professor
Modern Greek Program
Department of Greek and Latin
Ohio State University
Columbus, Ohio

Blue Earth Books

an imprint of Capstone Press
Mankato, Minnesota

Blue Earth Books are published by Capstone Press
151 Good Counsel Drive, P.O. Box 669, Mankato, Minnesota 56002
http://www.capstone-press.com

Library of Congress Cataloging-in-Publication Data
DeAngelis, Gina.
    Greece / by Gina DeAngelis.
    v. cm.—(Many cultures, one world)
    Includes bibliographical references and index.
    Contents: Welcome to Greece—A Greek legend—City and country life—Seasons in Greece—Family life in Greece—Laws, rules, and
customs—Pets in Greece—Sites to see in Greece.
    ISBN 0–7368–2167–8 (hardcover)
    1. Greece—Juvenile literature. [1. Greece.] I. Title. II. Series.
DF717.D43 2004
949.5—dc21   2002155268

Summary: An introduction to the geography, culture, and people of Greece, including a map, legend, recipe, craft, and game.

Editorial credits
Editor: Katy Kudela
Series Designer: Kia Adams
Photo Researcher: Alta Schaffer
Product Planning Editor: Karen Risch

Cover photo of Parga Greece, by PhotoDisc Inc./Colin Paterson

Artistic effects
James H. Miller, USDA Forest Service

Photo credits
AP/Wide World Photos/Eurokinissi, Antonis Nikolopoulos, 16
Blaine Harrington III, 29 (right)
Capstone Press, 23 (bottom); Gary Sundermeyer, 3 (middle, bottom),
    19 (right), 21, 25
Corbis/Bettmann, 8–9; Reuters NewMedia Inc., 15 (right); Gail Mooney, 17;
    Wolfgang Kaehler, 18–19
Houserstock/Dave G. Houser, 4–5; Jan Butchofsky-Houser, 13 (right)
Index Stock Imagery/Rick Strange, 14–15; Tina Buckman, 26, 27
National Academy of Design, New York/Bridgeman Art Library, 11
One Mile Up Inc., 23 (top)
SuperStock, 22–23
TRIP/H. Rogers, 28–29
The Viesti Collection Inc./Walter Bibikow, 6, 12–13; Joe Englander, 20;
    Joe Viesti, 24

1 2 3 4 5 6 08 07 06 05 04 03

Contents

Turn to page 7 to find a map of Greece.

Look on page 17 to learn a game many Greek children enjoy.

Check out page 21 to find out how to make a Greek dipping sauce.

See page 25 to learn how to make Greek Easter eggs.

CHAPTER 1

Welcome to Greece

Mountains, rich valleys, and rocky islands make up the country of Greece. More than 1,400 islands surround the peninsula-shaped country. Beautiful mountain ranges stretch across most of Greece's land. Mount Olympus is Greece's highest mountain. It stands 9,570 feet (2,917 meters) high.

Long ago, Greeks believed that gods and goddesses lived on Mount Olympus. Ancient Greeks told stories about the gods and goddesses who ruled the universe.

4

Facts about Greece

Name: ....Hellenic Republic

Capital: ....Athens

Population: ....More than 10 million people

Size: ....50,944 square miles

.........................(131,945 square kilometers)

Language: ....Greek

Religion: ....Christianity (Greek Orthodox)

Highest point: ....Mount Olympus, 9,570 feet

.........................(2,917 meters)

Lowest point: ....Mediterranean Sea, sea level

Main crops: ....Olives, tobacco

Money: ....Euro

Zeus (ZOOSS) was king of all the Greek gods. The city of Athens was named for the Greek goddess Athena. She was the goddess of wisdom. Ancient Greeks believed Athena gave the first olive tree to Earth.

Athens is Greece's largest city. It is also the country's capital. Athens is sometimes called the "birthplace of democracy." It was the first place where people elected their leaders.

Greece is a small country in southern Europe. It is a little smaller than the U.S. state of Alabama. No part of Greece is more than 85 miles (137 kilometers) from the sea. Greece's nearest neighbors are Italy, Albania, the Former Yugoslav Republic of Macedonia, Bulgaria, and Turkey.

Athens is the capital of Greece. Overlooking the city of Athens is an ancient Greek temple called the Parthenon.

Map of Greece

BULGARIA

FORMER YUGOSLAV REPUBLIC OF MACEDONIA

ALBANIA

ITALY

● Thessaloníki

Mount Olympus

G R E E C E

Aegean Sea

TURKEY

★ Athens

Mediterranean Sea

Legend

★ Capital City

● City

▲ Mountain

N
W   E
S

Crete

CHAPTER 2

A Greek Legend

Stories of gods and goddesses helped ancient Greeks explain nature. The story of Helios (HEE-lee-ohss) taught how the sun rose and set each day. Helios was the sun god. People believed that each morning he drove his chariot across the sky. Helios began his trip in the eastern sky. When Helios' chariot reached the western sky, the sun set.

Helios drove his chariot across the sky each morning.

Legends are stories handed down from earlier times. Legends often contain some truth but are mostly make-believe. Many Greek legends are well-known around the world. The legend of Hades (HAY-deez) and Persephone (pur-SEF-uh-nee) explains why the seasons change.

The Changing Seasons

Long ago, when the Earth was still young, flowers bloomed every day. Fields of wheat and orchards with fruit trees covered the land. Demeter (de-MEE-tur), the goddess of the harvest, watched over the land.

Demeter had a beautiful daughter named Persephone. Persephone helped her mother watch over the land.

Hades, the god of the Underworld, lived deep below the Earth. Hades was lonely. Life in the Underworld was dark and unpleasant.

One day, Hades caught sight of Persephone working in the fields with her mother. He immediately fell in love with the young girl. Hades wanted Persephone to be queen of the Underworld. He believed her beauty would brighten his days.

Hades jumped into his chariot and had his driver take him up to Earth's surface. He grabbed Persephone and took her down to the Underworld.

Demeter was very sad. She ordered the Earth to stop growing. The trees and grasses quickly died away. The cattle and sheep no longer had food. Soon, people on Earth began to starve.

Hearing the cries of the people, Zeus decided to do something. He ordered Hades to return Persephone to her mother. But Hades did not want to lose his beautiful bride. He tricked Persephone into eating six seeds from a pomegranate. This fruit was the food of the Underworld. By tasting this fruit, Persephone could not leave the Underworld.

Zeus was angry when he heard this news. He knew Persephone was trapped forever in the Underworld. Zeus quickly thought up a plan that would keep both Hades and Demeter happy.

Persephone stayed with Demeter for six months of the year. This time became summer when plants grew and blossomed. After a six-month visit, Persephone returned to the Underworld. During these six months, the Earth grew cold and the plants died. This season became known as winter.

Hades and his chariot driver rode up to
Earth's surface to meet Persephone.

CHAPTER 3

City and Country Life

Many Greeks live in Athens, Thessaloníki, or other large cities. It costs a lot to live in these cities. Large apartments fill city blocks.

Some Greeks live in small towns or in farming villages. Farmers in these villages grow olives, grains, fruit, and vegetables.

Different areas in Greece have different styles of houses. In the northern mountains, rooftops are slanted. This slant keeps heavy snow from collecting. In southern Greece, people paint their houses white. This color reflects the hot sunlight and keeps houses cooler.

Many apartments line the city streets of Greece.

People living in the countryside use donkeys to carry heavy loads.

13

CHAPTER 4

Seasons in Greece

Greece is located along the Mediterranean Sea. This body of water lies between southern Europe and northern Africa. Mediterranean summers are hot and dry.

Greece is a country with warm, sunny weather most of the year. In southern Greece, summer temperatures can reach 99 degrees Fahrenheit (37 degrees Celsius). But temperatures in Greece change with the area. Summer temperatures in northern Greece are cooler. The mountain areas

People in Greece enjoy the warm weather and sandy beaches.

Olympic Games

A worldwide Summer Olympics and a Winter Olympics are held every four years. Athletes from around the world participate in these games.

The Olympics began in ancient Greece. Every four years, ancient Greeks gathered together for a festival called the Olympic Games. These games were held in late summer. The Olympic Games included races, boxing and wrestling contests, and other sporting events. The Olympic Games were so important that wars stopped while the games were held.

The Olympic Games will return to Athens, Greece, in 2004.

This logo represents the 2004 Olympic Games in Athens, Greece.

reach about 77 degrees Fahrenheit (25 degrees Celsius).

Winters in the Mediterranean area are cool and wet. Greece's winter season begins around mid-October and ends in mid-March. Winter temperatures are cool. The average winter temperature in Greece is 59 degrees Fahrenheit (15 degrees Celsius).

The winter season sometimes brings snow to central Greece.

Flees

Greece's warm weather makes it perfect for outdoor activities and sports. Children in Greece spend much of their time outdoors. Many enjoy playing the game Flees.

What You Need

five or more players
playground ball

What You Do

1. Players form a circle.
2. Choose one player to stand in the center of the circle.
3. The player in the center of the circle throws the ball in the air and shouts the name of another player.
4. The player whose name is called must catch the ball. Meanwhile, the other players scatter.
5. The player who catches the ball counts to three. On the count of three, all the players must stop moving.
6. The player with the ball must try to hit as many players with the ball as possible.
7. If the thrower misses, the game starts over.
8. Each player may only receive five hits, called flees. When a player receives five flees they are out of the game.
9. The player who stays in the game the longest is the winner.

CHAPTER 5

Family Life in Greece

Greek children often go on outings with their cousins. Greek families are very close to their relatives.

Most parents in Greece have only two children, but relatives often live near each other. Children grow up close to their aunts, uncles, cousins, and grandparents. This tight group of relatives is called a "kin." People in Greece also have groups of close friends called "paréa."

Many Greeks work in family-owned businesses such as grocery stores and restaurants. Every member of the family helps with the business.

Birthdays in Greece

Children in Greece often celebrate birthdays with a cake. Many people believe the idea of a birthday cake came from ancient Greece. Ancient Greeks made cakes as offerings to the goddess of the moon. These cakes were round like a full moon. Later, candles were added to make the cakes glow like a full moon.

Meals are a time for Greek families to gather together. Greeks eat their main meal in the afternoon. Lamb is a favorite meat to serve. People in Greece also enjoy seafood and fish caught from the Mediterranean Sea. They flavor their foods with olive oil and herbs.

Greek meals offer many foods. Most Greek dishes include fresh vegetables, such as cucumbers and eggplant. Fresh fruit, olives, and feta cheese also are served at most meals. Sweet pastries such as baklava may be served for dessert.

Shops in Greece sell sweet pastries and other baked goods.

Tzatziki

Yogurt is a popular food in Greece. Greeks eat yogurt with honey and fruit. They also use yogurt in many of their recipes. A favorite Greek recipe is called tzatziki. This dip combines the Greeks' love of fresh herbs and vegetables with yogurt. Greeks take pride in serving foods made with fresh ingredients.

What You Need

Ingredients
1 cucumber, seeded and cut into small chunks
¼ teaspoon (1.2 mL) garlic powder
1 teaspoon (5 mL) olive oil
1 teaspoon (5 mL) dried dill
1 cup (240 mL) plain yogurt
vegetables

Equipment
small mixing bowl
measuring spoons
wooden spoon
dry-ingredient measuring cup
plastic wrap

What You Do

1. Mix cucumber pieces, garlic powder, olive oil, and dill together in small bowl.
2. Add the plain yogurt and mix well.
3. Cover the bowl with plastic wrap. Put the bowl in the refrigerator for at least 2 hours.
4. Serve the tzatziki as a dip for vegetables.

Makes about 1½ cups (360 mL) of dip

CHAPTER 6

Laws, Rules, and Customs

Greece invented the democratic form of government. The word democracy means "rule by the people." In a democracy, people vote for someone to act for them in government. The prime minister heads Greece's government. Greek citizens elect 300 people to represent them in government.

Greece is well-known for its ways of learning. Many great philosophers came from ancient Greece. Today, Greek law says all children must attend school from the ages of 6 to 15. Greek children attend elementary

Greek children must attend school for at least nine years.

Greece's national flag is blue and white. The five blue stripes stand for the sky and the sea. The four white stripes stand for the purity of Greece's fight for freedom. A white cross in the top left corner represents Greek Orthodox Christianity.

People in Greece use the euro. In 2000, Greece began using this money. Euros come in notes and coins. One hundred cents equals one euro.

23

school for six years. The next three years of school are called "gymnasium."

Students who continue their studies attend "lykeio." After three years, students may graduate. Following lykeio, students may attend a university. Some students find a job instead of continuing their education.

Religion is an important part of life in Greece. Today, most people in Greece follow the Greek Orthodox Christian religion.

Easter is the most celebrated holiday in Greece. On Easter Sunday, people attend church services. Later, families gather together for family dinners.

Greeks often dress in traditional clothes on Easter Sunday. Many Greeks walk together to church on Easter Sunday.

Greek Easter Eggs

Each year on the Thursday before Easter Sunday, people in Greece dye red Easter eggs. Christians believe Jesus died on the cross. The red dye is a symbol of his blood.

On Easter Sunday, Greek families place the red dyed hard-boiled eggs on their feast tables. Everyone takes an egg and clinks it against everyone else's eggs. The person whose egg breaks last is believed to have good luck.

What You Need

old newspapers
package of red egg dye
small bowl
paper cup
a dozen hard-boiled eggs
timer
spoon
wire cooling rack
empty egg carton
paper towel
1 teaspoon (5 mL) olive oil

What You Need

1. Place old newspapers on a countertop or table where you plan to dye eggs. The newspapers will keep the workspace clean.
2. Prepare the red egg dye in small bowl according to package directions.
3. Carefully fill the paper cup halfway with red egg dye.
4. Using a spoon, carefully place an egg in the paper cup.
5. Using a timer, allow the egg to sit for at least 5 minutes.
6. Carefully remove the egg from the dye with a spoon. Allow the egg to dry on a wire rack. After the egg has dried, store it in the egg carton.
7. Repeat steps 4, 5, and 6 with the other eggs.
8. When the eggs have dried, rub the eggs with a paper towel dipped in olive oil. The olive oil gives the eggs a shiny look.
9. The eggs can be eaten as a snack or as part of a meal. Store eggs in refrigerator until ready to eat.

CHAPTER 7

Pets in Greece

People in Greece keep animals to do a job. Some people have a dog or a cat. A dog may be used to guard a house, while a cat can catch mice. Many people in the country keep donkeys to carry heavy loads and pull carts. But donkeys are not just work animals. People love their donkeys like other pets.

Homeless animals are a problem in Greece's large cities. Many cats and dogs roam city streets. They also gather at tourist sites to search for food. People are working to bring attention to these homeless animals.

Some people in Greece choose a dog for a pet.

Donkeys are an important animal in Greece. Many families treat their donkey as a family pet.

CHAPTER 8

Sites to See in Greece

On a rocky hilltop in Athens sits the ruins of a Greek temple. This white marble temple is called the Parthenon. The ancient Greeks built it thousands of years ago. Today, people visit Athens to see the temple's ruins.

Theater is an ancient Greek practice that is still popular today. Long ago, the ancient Greeks built arenas throughout the land. Greek plays lasted all day. During the summer, people continue to enjoy plays performed in these ancient arenas.

The Parthenon stands on a hilltop in Athens. This historic site gives people a view of ancient Greek building styles.

Long ago, ancient Greeks built arenas. Today, people still visit these arenas to watch plays.

Words to Know

ancient (AYN-shunt)—very old

chariot (CHA-ree-uht)—a light, two-wheeled cart pulled by horses

democracy (di-MOK-ruh-see)—a system of government in which citizens vote for their leaders

marble (MAR-bul)—hard stone used for making buildings

Olympic Games (oh-LIM-pik GAMES)—sports contests among athletes from many nations

Parthenon (PAHR-thuh-non)—ancient Greek temple located in Athens, Greece

philosopher (fuh-LOSS-uh-fer)—one who studies wisdom, truth, and ideas

pomegranate (POM-uh-gran-it)—a round, reddish yellow fruit

ruins (ROO-inz)—the remains of a building that has been destroyed

To Learn More

Britton, Tamara L. *Greece.* The Countries. Edina, Minn.: Abdo, 2000.

Petersen, Christine, and David Petersen. *Greece.* A True Book. New York: Children's Press, 2001.

Richardson, Adele D. *Hades.* World Mythology. Mankato, Minn.: Capstone Press, 2003.

Riehecky, Janet. *Greece.* Countries of the World. Mankato, Minn.: Bridgestone Books, 2001.

Useful Addresses

Embassy of Greece
2221 Massachusetts Avenue NW
Washington, DC 20008

Embassy of the Hellenic Republic
76-80 MacLaren Street
Ottawa, ON K2P 0K6
Canada

The Greek Institute
1038 Massachusetts Avenue
Cambridge, MA 02138

Greek National Tourist Organization
Olympic Tower
645 Fifth Avenue, Suite 903
New York, NY 10022

Internet Sites

Do you want to find out more about Greece?
Let FactHound, our fact-finding hound dog, do the research for you.

Here's how:

1) Visit *http://www.facthound.com*
2) Type in the **Book ID** number: **0736821678**
3) Click on **FETCH IT.**

**FactHound will fetch Internet sites picked
by our editors just for you!**

Index